YOUR KNOWLEDGE HAS VALUE

Christos-Athenagoras Ziliaskopoulos

Immigration, society and religion in Germany: The "Interfaith Council" in Frankfurt/Main

GRIN Publishing

Bibliographic information published by the German National Library:

The German National Library lists this publication in the National Bibliography;
detailed bibliographic data are available on the Internet at http://dnb.dnb.de .

Imprint:

Copyright © 2012 GRIN Verlag, Open Publishing GmbH
Print and binding: Books on Demand GmbH, Norderstedt Germany
ISBN: 978-3-656-18717-2

This book at GRIN:

http://www.grin.com/en/e-book/192881/immigration-society-and-religion-in-germa-
ny-the-interfaith-council

GRIN - Your knowledge has value

Since its foundation in 1998, GRIN has specialized in publishing academic texts by students, college teachers and other academics as e-book and printed book. The website www.grin.com is an ideal platform for presenting term papers, final papers, scientific essays, dissertations and specialist books.

Visit us on the internet:

http://www.grin.com/

http://www.facebook.com/grincom

http://www.twitter.com/grin_com

Christos-Athenagoras Ziliaskopoulos

Immigration, society and religion in Germany: The "Interfaith Council " in Frankfurt/Main.

An Essay

April 2012

Introduction

It is only after 1960´s immigration[1] has been framed negatively by Western European countries. A brief answer to the question why the view towards the immigrants changed in 1960´s could be the dissolution of the Eastern Block which caused enormous demographic changes which had as a consequence serious impact on socioeconomic level. The mobilization of a great mass of people lead European national states to ethnicise their migration policies in a way that encourage the arrival of immigrants from the simiral ethnic background, in order to achieve, a re-homogenization in the Post-Communist era (Kaya, 2011, 21). Immigrants of different cultural background rather that the majority´s were disapproved. Kaya (2011) in the very same article mentions that this massive migration flows was *parallel with the rise of heterophobic discourses such as the „clash of civilisations", „culture wars..."* (Kaya, 2011, 4).

Immigration in Germany

Specifically, on the German example, immigration inflow was considered a necessity for the rebuilt of a dilapidated Germany. Thus the Federal Labor Institute (FLI) in cooperation with the German authorities recruites foreign workers, in the late 1950´s and 1960´s numerous Treaties were signed with Spain, Greece, Turkey, Yugoslavia, Portugal. The foreign workers were under the status of "guest workers" implying that their presence in Germany was temporal (Constant, Nottmeyer, Zimmermann, 2009, 2).

Germany failed on the re-patriation process of the „guest process" which ended being permanent residents in the host country. Constant, Nottmeyer, Zimmermann (2009) in their article mention that in the 1980´s and earlz 1990´s the immigration boosted by asylum seekers and „ethnic Germans" which were coming to Germany in the aftermath

---

[1] In an initial attempt to theorize immigration policy, Meyers's (2000) point rise a very crusial argument that immigration is not well defined and lacks, fort he most part, attempts to debate the relative merits of various schools of thought on the subject (Meyers, 2010, 1246). Under the discipline of Political Sciences immigration policy had been analyzed via the Marxist, –presented by Beard and Beard (1944),Gorz (1970), Marshall (1973),Marx (1973, 1976),Castells (1975),Nikolinakos (1975), Castles and Kosack (1985), Miles (1986, 1987, 1989) and Bovenkerk et al. (1990, 1991)- interest group, partisan politics and institutionalist approaches, additionally the field of international relations has added to the concept via the analysis from the realism, liberalism and world system approaches and under the discipline of sociology and psychology, immigration has been also examined via the national identity approach.

of the fall of the iron Curtaindue to liberalized travel regulations. Immigration of the latter, the so-called „Aussiedler" from Poland, Romania, and the former Soviet Union, increased until a new more restrictive law was enforced in 1993. (Constant, Nottmeyer, Zimmermann, 2009, 3).

Despite the great inflow of immigrant population in Germany, today according the Federal Statistics Office, approximately 18% of the population of Germany are either without German citizenship (8%) or German citizenship holders of immigrant background (10%)[2]- as Radtke (1994, 2003) argues:

Against statistical evidence, Germany in the second half of the twentieth century reluctantly denied being an immigrant country. For years, multiculturalism was nothing more than a mere discourse in the political arena and the media, brought forward as an argument by those in competing political parties, in churches and welfare organisations who attempted to initiate a re-description of the dominating jus-sanguinis-based self-concept of the nation. Their political and pedagogical intention was to advocate the recognition of ethnic diversity and to upgrade the integration of immigrants to a major task of the administrations at all federal levels. (Radtke, 2003, 56).

It is a considerably recent attempt for the German national authorities to move integration to a policy concern and establish a new civil and social identidy for all citizens. Religious and cultural identidy are most then ever important in postmodern history of Germany. The new immigration law which was introduced on 2005 has serious amentments for the integration process Heckmann (2010), while refering to the new immigration law mentions „integration in Germany has not been left primarily to the market and civil society processes" and he continues arguing on the widely accepted notion that „integration happens at the local level that local policies have been responded to the new challenges by making integration policies a top priority" (Heckmann, 2010, 2-3).

---

[2]http://www.destatis.de/jetspeed/portal/cms/Sites/destatis/Internet/EN/Content/Statistics/Bevoelkerung/A uslaendischeBevoelkerung/Tabellen/Content50/TOP10Liste,templateId=renderPrint.psml

The Interfaith Council[3] in Frankfurt

Frankfurt's Interfaith Council (Rat der Religionen)[4], created on April 1. 2009, acts cooperatively with the local authorities of the city of Frankfurt. The Council counts 23 members, all are representative of their religious communities (Gemeinde). More precisely, the 23 members are representing 9 religious communities: Christians, Judishs, Muslims, Budhists, Hindus, Sihks, Bahais, Ahmadiyya Muslims and Mormons.

The purpose and the objectives of the Council as they are declared in the statement of its creation are:

§ 2 Purpose and Objectives

First

The purpose of the Council is the promotion of religion by the dialogue between them. The aim will be achieved through: 1. Guidance to member communities and other religious communities, 2. Cooperation with the municipal institutions, and government agencies, associations, institutions and societies in the city, 3. Seminars, conferences, publications, interfaith events and projects.

---

[3] Great is the debate around the identity as well, but identity theories pre-suppose the elaboration with the social representation theories thus it should be added that the notion of social representation counts more than twenty years in social psychology and it is inherent in social sciences too. The first who introduced the concept of social representation was Moscovici (1961) who was inspired by the work of Emile Durkheim's and his concept of collective consciousness (Andrianou; 2004: 6). The concept of identity appeared in psychology with Erikson (1950), who introduced the triple separation of identity. According to his study "the distinction rested on the ego identity (sometimes identified simply as "the self"); the personal idiosyncrasies that separate one person from the next, known as the personal identity; and the collection of social roles that a person might play, known as either the social identity or the cultural identity" (Cote & Levine; 2002: 22). According to Breakwell (1992), "Social identity theory, while it attempts to explain intergroup relationships, is a model that focuses upon individual needs and motivation (the need for a positive social identity) as the means of fundamentally explaining inter-personal and intergroup dynamics" (Breakwell; 1993: 1). In identity theory the position of memory is very important as well, Assmann (1995) attributes several characteristics to cultural memory, firstly, noting that it is characterized "by its distance from everyday." (Assmann; 1995: 129) Assmann prolongs referring that: *Distance from the everyday (transcendence) marks its temporal horizon. Cultural memory has its fixed point; its horizon does not change with the passing of time. These fixed points are fateful events of the past, whose memory is maintained through cultural formation (texts, rites, monuments) and institutional communication (recitation, practice, observance). We call these "figures of memory".* (Assmann; 1995: 129).Ethnic identity has traditionally been most salient in immigrant receiving countries like USA and Australia, but it has become an increasingly important issue throughout the world, as social and political changes have increased the amount of contact among people from different ethnic groups and, in some cases, have led to ethnic conflict. (Phinney; 2001: 4821 in the Encyclopedia of Social Sciences).

[4] http://www.rat-der-religionen.de/index.html

Second

The Council aims to: The Council is concerned with social and political issues in the city and takes a position on issues of coexistence[5]. The Council encourages contact, networking and mutual understanding among religions represented in Frankfurt. This support of inter-religious dialogue should be, also in cooperation with the municipality have a positive impact on reducing conflict and coexistence and send important signals to the local communities and the urban public.[6]

Despite the cooperation with the local authorities the *Interfaith Council of Frankfurt* was a product of civil society. It emerged from the need for a peacefull coexistence from and for the citizens of Frankfurt . Critical could be considered the question why is there a need for such an organization to promote the mutual understanding of the different religious groups in Frankfurt and what was prohibbiting the mutual understanding and peaceful co-existance?

In an era when there is a tendency to blame multiculturalism[7] for causing ethnic

---

[5] The „theologico-political problem" as it was first intoduced by Strauss (1997) states that the problem is merely one that of authority. Eberle and Cuneo mention on their article: The standard view among political theorists, such as Robert Audi, Jürgen Habermas, Charles Larmore, Steven Macedo, Martha Nussbaum, and John Rawls is that religious reasons can play only a limited role in justifying coercive laws, as coercive laws that require a religious rationale lack moral legitimacy. (Eberle, Cuneo, 2008, 4). Although, secularism has played a tremendous role in post-modernity in the democratization process the relations of state and church are still a great field of research.

[6] § 2 Zweck und Ziele: 1. Der Zweck des Rates ist die Förderung von Religionen durch den Dialog zwischen ihnen. Der Zweck wird verwirklicht durch: 1. Beratung der Mitgliedsgemeinschaften und anderer Religionsgemeinschaften, 2. Zusammenarbeit mit den städtischen Einrichtungen, sowie Behörden, Vereinen, Institutionen und Gesellschaften in der Stadt, 3. Seminare, Tagungen, Veröffentlichungen, interreligiöse Veranstaltungen und Projekte. 2. Der Rat verfolgt folgende Ziele: Der Rat beschäftigt sich mit gesellschaftlichen und politischen Themen in der Stadt und nimmt Stellung zu Fragen des Zusammenlebens. Der Rat fördert den Kontakt, die Vernetzung und das gegenseitige Verständnis unter den in Frankfurt vertretenen Religionen. Diese Unterstützung des interreligiösen Dialogs soll sich, auch in Zusammenarbeit mit der Kommune, positiv und konfliktreduzierend auf das Zusammenleben auswirken und wichtige Signale an die örtlichen Gemeinden und die Stadtöffentlichkeit senden. (http://www.rat-der-religionen.de/satzung.html).

[7] Song (2010) argues that multiculturalism is a body of thought in political philosophy about proper way to respond to cultural and religious diversity. The term has been associated with „identity politics", „the politics of difference", but it is also a topic for economic and political power interest. Numerous scholars attributed thoughts to this body, not surpringly multiculturalism has tight bonds with antiracism, as Blum (1992) mentions: "the former highlights "cultural life, cultural expression, achievements, and the like whereas the latter victimization and resistance" (Blum 1992, 14). Multiculturalism found its supporters in Communitarian, Liberal Egalitarian, Postcolonial persperctives but the critiques were not few as well. One of the most interesting argument towards multiculturalism was recently introduced and refers to the problematic of „internal minorities"(Green 1994, Eisenberg and Spinner-Halev 2005), quoting Song (2010): Some of the most oppressive group norms and practices revolve around issues of gender and sexuality, and many feminist critics have highlighted the tensions between multiculturalism and feminism (Okin 1999, Shachar 2000). This is a genuine dilemma

tensions[8] and Islamophobia, immigrantophobia, antisionism, neonazism and xenophobia has risen, the creation of a council based on the ideological background of multiclturalism, equality and mutual respect is of extremely important. The Interfaith Council of Frankfurt promotes integration. He recognizes the value of the enrichment through immigration and the challenge that Diaspora[9] brings to Germany. The interreligious dialogue is perceived form different religious groups and gives religious communities a place in a modern society and provides the democratization process in a secular state.

---

if one accepts both that group-differentiated rights for minority cultural groups are justifiable, as multicultural theorists do, and that gender equality is an important value, as feminists have emphasized. Extending special protections and accommodations to patriarchal cultural communities may help reinforce gender inequality within these communities. Examples include conflicts over polygamy, arranged marriage, the ban on headscarves in France, "cultural defenses" in criminal law, accommodating religious law or customary law within the dominant legal system, and self-government rights for indigenous communities that deny equality to women in certain respects (Deveaux 2006, Phillips 2007, Shachar 2001, Song 2007).

[8] Language, religion, ethnicity enclose inside them aspects of figures of memory which are fixed. Nations, regions, ethnic groups, local communities are caring fateful events of the past in order to formulate a sense of common belonging. Phinney (2001) The Encyclopedia of Social Sciences determines ethnic identity as: (...) a dynamic, multidimensional construct that refers to one's identity, or sense of self, as a member of an ethnic group. An ethnic group can be thought of as a subgroup within a larger context that claims a common ancestry and shares one or more of the following elements: culture, race, religion, language, kinship, and place of origin. Ethnic identity is a central defining characteristic of many individuals, particularly those who are members of minority or lower status groups (Liebkind 1992, Phinney 1990).

[9] The movement across national and cultural borders brings up more violently the issue of group identity. The sense of difference becomes more obvious when "one" assembles the "other", thus refugees, immigrants, guest workers, are themselves carriers of a certain identity, which creates questions to both mobile groups and receiving groups. Although Diaspora as a concept was bond with the forcible dispersion of the Jewish people, the term has also implications to modern types of migration thus as Cohen (2001) implies "the key difference between "Diaspora" and more popularly recognized forms of migration is that in the first case cultural, linguistic, religious, historical, and affective ties with the place of origin remain strong. In the second, at least in theory immigration from "an old country" involves a one-way ticket, assimilation to the "new country", the adoption of a local citizenship and language, and the public acceptance of local ways and customs." (Cohen; 2001: 3643 in the Encyclopedia of Social Sciences).

References/ Bibliography

- Anderson, E., 1999, "What is the Point of Equality?" *Ethics,* 109(2): 287–337.
- Appiah, A., 2005, *The Ethics of Identity,* Princeton: Princeton University Press.
- Benhabib, S., 2002, *The Claims of Culture: Equality and Diversity in the Global Era,* Princeton: Princeton University Press.
- Bowen, J.R., 2007, *Why the French Don't Like Headscarves: Islam, the State, and Public Space,* Princeton: Princeton University Press.
- Carens, J., 2000, *Culture, Citizenship, and Community: A Contexual Exploration of Justice as Evenhandedness,* Oxford: Oxford University Press.
- Deveaux, M., 2006, *Gender and Justice in Multicultural Liberal States,* Oxford: Oxford University Press.
- Eisenberg, A., 2003, "Diversity and Equality: Three Approaches to Cultural and Sexual Difference," *Journal of Political Philosophy,* 11(1): 41–64.
- —— and J. Spinner-Halev (eds.), 2005, *Minorities within Minorities: Equality, Rights, and Diversity,* Cambridge: Cambridge University Press.
- Fraser, N., & A. Honneth, 2003, *Redistribution or Recognition? A Political-philosophical Exchange,* London: Verso.
- Friedman, M., 2003, *Autonomy, Gender, Politics,* Oxford: Oxford University Press.
- Gooding-Williams, R., 1998, "Race, Multiculturalism and Democracy," *Constellations,* 5(1): 18–41.
- Green, L., 1994, "Internal Minorities and Their Rights," in *Group Rights,* J. Baker (ed.), Toronto: University of Toronto Press, pp. 101–117.
- Gutmann, A., 2003, *Identity in Democracy,* Princeton: Princeton University Press.
- Hollinger, D., 1995, *Postethnic America: Beyond Multiculturalism,* New York: Basic Books.
- Ivison, D., 2006, "Historical Injustice," in *The Oxford Handbook of Political Theory,* J. Dryzek, B. Honig, and A. Phillips (eds.), Oxford: Oxford University Press, 507–25.

- Ivison, D., P. Patton, and W. Sanders, 2000, *Political Theory and the Rights of Indigenous Peoples,* Cambridge: Cambridge University Press.
- Johnson, J., 2000, "Why Respect Culture?" *American Journal of Political Science,* 44(3): 405–418.
- Jones, P., 1994, "Bearing the Consequences of Belief," *Journal of Political Philosophy,* 2(1): 24–43.
- Kelly, P., 2002 , *Multiculturalism Reconsidered: Culture and Equality and Its Critics,* Oxford: Polity Press.
- Kukathas, C., 1995, "Are There Any Cultural Rights?" *Political Theory,* 20: 105–139.
- ——, 2003, *The Liberal Archipelago: A Theory of Diversity and Freedom,* Oxford: Oxford University Press.
- Kymlicka, W. 1989, *Liberalism, Community, and Culture,* Oxford: Oxford University Press.
- ——, 1995, *Multicultural Citizenship: A Liberal Theory of Minority Rights,* Oxford: Oxford University Press.
- ——(ed.), 1995, *The Rights of Minority Cultures,* Oxford: Oxford University Press.
- ——, 1999, "Liberal Complacencies", in *Is Multiculturalism Bad for Women?* J. Cohen and M. Howard, and M.C. Nussbaum (eds.), Princeton: Princeton University Press.
- ——, 2001, *Politics in the Vernacular: Nationalism, Multiculturalism, and Citizenship*, Oxford: Oxford University Press.
- —— and A. Patten, 2003, *Language Rights and Political Theory,* Oxford: Oxford University Press.
- Laborde, C., 2008, *Critical Republicanism: The Hijab Controversy and Political Philosophy*, Oxford: Oxford University Press.
- Levy, J.T., 1997, "Classifying Cultural Rights," *Nomos XXXIX: Ethnicity and Group Rights,* W. Kymlicka and I. Shapiro (eds.), New York: New York University Press.
- ——, 2000, *Multiculturalism of Fear*, Oxford: Oxford University Press.

- Means, A., 2002, "Narrative Argumentation: Arguing with Natives," *Constellations,* 9(2): 221–245.
- Miller, D., 2002, "Liberalism, Equal Opportunities and Cultural Commitments," in *Multicultural Reconsidered: Culture and Equality and Its Critics,* P. Kelly (ed.), Oxford: Polity Press.
- Modood, T., 1998, "Anti-Essentialism, Multiculturalism, and the 'Recognition' of Religious Groups," *Journal of Political Philosophy,* 6(4): pp?
- Moore, M., 2005, "Internal Minorities and Indigenous Self-Determination," in *Minorities within Minorities: Equality, Rights and Diversity,* A. Eisenberg and J. Spinner-Halev (eds.), Cambridge: Cambridge University Press.
- Okin, S., 1999, "Is Multiculturalism Bad for Women?" in *Is Multiculturalism Bad for Women?* J. Cohen, M. Howard, and M.C. Nussbaum (eds.), Princeton: Princeton University Press.
- ——, 2005, "Multiculturalism and Feminism: No Simple Questions, No Simple Answers," in *Minorities within Minorities: Equality, Rights, and Diversity,* A. Eisenberg and J. Spinner-Halev (eds.), Cambridge: Cambridge University Press.
- Parekh, B., 2000, *Rethinking Multiculturalism: Cultural Diversity and Political Theory,* Cambridge, MA: Harvard University Press.
- Patten, A., 2001, "The Rights of Internal Linguistic Minorities," in *Minorities within Minorities: Equality, Rights and Diversity,* A. Eisenberg and J. Spinner-Halev (eds.), Cambridge: Cambridge University Press.
- Phillips, A., 2007, *Multiculturalism without Culture.* Princeton, NJ: Princeton University Press.
- Scheffler, S., 2001, "Conceptions of Cosmopolitanism," in *Boundaries and Allegiances: Problems of Justice and Responsibility in Liberal Thought,* Oxford: Oxford University Press.
- ——, 2003, "What is Egalitarianism?" *Philosophy and Public Affairs* 31(1): 5–39.
- ——, 2007, "Immigration and the Significance of Culture," *Philosophy and Public Affairs,* 35(2): 93–125.
- Shachar, A., 2000, "On Citizenship and Mulicultural Vulnerability," *Political Theory,* 28: 64–89.

- ——, 2001, *Multicultural Jurisdictions: Cultural Differences and Women's Rights,* Cambridge: Cambridge University Press.
- Simpson, A., 2000, "Paths toward a Mohawk Nation: Narratives of Citizenship and Nationhood in Kahnawake," in *Political Theory and the Rights of Indigenous Peoples,* D. Ivison, P. Patton, and W. Sanders (eds.), Cambridge: Cambridge University Press.
- Song, S., 2007, *Justice, Gender, and the Politics of Multiculturalism,* Cambridge: Cambridge University Press.
- ——, 2008, "The Subject of Multiculturalism: Culture, Religion, Language, Ethnicity, Nationality, and Race?" in *New Waves in Political Philosophy,* B. de Bruin and C. Zurn (eds.), New York: Palgrave MacMillan.
- Spinner-Halev, J., 1994, *Surviving Diversity: Religion and Democratic Citizenship,* Baltimore: Johns Hopkins University Press.
- Taylor, C., 1992, "The Politics of Recognition," in *Multiculturalism: Examining the Politics of Recognition,* A. Gutmann (ed.), Princeton: Princeton University Press.
- ——, 1995, "Irreducibly Social Goods,", in *Philosophical Arguments,* Cambridge, MA: Harvard University Press.
- Tully, J., 1995, *Strange Multiplicity: Constitutionalism in an Age of Diversity,* Cambridge: Cambridge University Press.
- Waldron, J., 1992, "Superseding Historic Injustice," *Ethics,* 103(1): 4–28.
- ——, 1995, "Minority Cultures and the Cosmopolitan Alternative," in *The Rights of Minority Cultures,* Oxford: Oxford University Press.
- Williams, M., 1998, *Voice, Trust, and Memory: Marginalized Groups and the Failings of Liberal Representation,* Princeton: Princeton University Press.
- Young, I.M., 1990, *Justice and the Politics of Difference,* Princeton, NJ: Princeton University Press.
- Ackerman, Bruce. 1989. "Why Dialogue?" *Journal of Philosophy* 86: 5-22.
- Audi, Robert. 2000. *Religious Commitment and Secular Reason.* Cambridge University Press.

- ——. 1997. "Liberal Democracy and the Place of Religion in Politics." In Robert Audi and Nicholas Wolterstorff. *Religion in the Public Square*. Lanham, MD: Rowman and Littlefield: 1-66.

- Berger, Peter. 1986. "The Story of an Encounter." In Richard John Neuhaus, ed. *Unsecular America*. Grand Rapids, MI: Eerdmans: 67-114.

- ——. 1969. *The Sacred Canopy: Elements of a Sociological Theory of Religion*. Garden City, NJ: Anchor Books.

- Berman, Paul. 2003. *Terror and Liberalism*. New York: W.W. Norton.

- Boettcher, James. 2007. "Respect, Recognition, and Public Reason." *Social Theory and Practice* 33: 223-49.

- Burleigh, Michael. 2005. *Earthly Powers: The Clash of Religion and Politics in Europe, from the French Revolution to the Great War*. New York: Harper Perennial.

- ——. 2007. *Sacred Causes: The Clash of Religion and Politics, from the Great War to the War on Terror*. New York: Harper Perennial.

- Carter, Stephen. 1993. *The Culture of Disbelief*. New York: Basic Books.

- Cuneo, Terence, ed. 2005. *Religion in the Liberal Polity*. Notre Dame, IN: Notre Dame University Press.

- Digeser, Elizabeth DePalma. 2000. *The Making of a Christian Empire: Lactantius and Rome*. Ithaca, NY: Cornell University Press.

- Eberle, Christopher. 2006. "Religion, Pacifism and the Doctrine of Restraint." *Journal of Religious Ethics* 34: 203-24.

- ——. 2005. "What Does Respect Require?" In Cuneo (2005): 173-94.

- ——. 2002. *Religious Conviction in Liberal Politics*. Cambridge University Press.

- Finke, Roger and Rodney Stark. 2000. *Acts of Faith: Explaining the Human Side of Religion*. Berkeley, CA: University of California Press.

- Jackson, Timothy. 1997. "The Return of the Prodigal? Liberal Theory and Religious Pluralism." In Weithman (1997): 182-217.

- Gaus, Gerald. Forthcoming. "The Place of Religious Belief in Public Reasons Liberalism." In Maria Dimova-Cookson and Peter Stirk, eds. *Multiculturalism and Moral Conflict*, London: Routledge

- ——. 1996. *Justificatory Liberalism.* Oxford University Press.
- Greenawalt, Kent. 2004. *Does God Belong in the Public Schools?* Princeton, NJ: Princeton University Press.
- ——. 1995. *Private Consciences and Public Reasons.* Oxford University Press.
- ——. 1988. *Religious Conviction and Political Choice.* Oxford University Press.
- Greene, Abner. 1993. "The Political Balance of the Religion Clauses." *Yale Law Journal* 102: 1619-44.
- Gutmann, Amy and Dennis Thompson. 1996. *Democracy and Disagreement.* Cambridge, MA: Harvard University Press.
- Habermas, Jürgen. 2006. "Religion in the Public Sphere." *European Journal of Philosophy* 14: 1-25
- Hill, Christopher. 1994. *The English Bible and the Seventeenth-Century Revolution.* London: Penguin Books.
- Langerak, Edward. 2007. "Religion in the Public Square." *Philosophy Compass* 2: 129-40.
- ——. 1996. "Theism and Toleration." In Philip Quinn and Charles Taliaferro, eds., *A Companion to the Philosophy of Religion.* Oxford: Blackwell: 514-24.
- Larmore, Charles. 1987. *Patterns of Moral Complexity.* Cambridge University Press.
- Locke, John. 1983. *A Letter Concerning Toleration.* Edited by James Tully. Indianapolis, IN: Hackett.
- Macedo, Stephen. 1990. "The Politics of Justification." *Political Theory* 18: 280-304.
- MacIntyre, Alasdair. 1990. *Three Rival Versions of Moral Inquiry.* Notre Dame, IN: Notre Dame University Press.
- ——. 1988. *Whose Justice? Which Rationality?* Notre Dame, IN: Notre Dame University Press.
- ——. 1984. *After Virtue*, 2nd edn. Notre Dame, IN: Notre Dame University Press.
- ——. 1983. "Are There Any Natural Rights?: The Charles F. Adams Lecture of February 28, 1983." Published by Bowdoin College, Bowdoin, Maine.
- Milbank, John. 1990. *Theology and Social Theory: Beyond Secular Reason.* Oxford: Blackwell.

- Milbank, John, Catherine Pickstock, and Graham Ward, eds. 1999. *Radical Orthodoxy: A New Theology*. London: Routledge.
- Moffett, Samuel Hugh. 1986. *A History of Christianity in Asia: Beginnings to 1500*. Maryknoll, NY: Orbis Books.
- Mouw, Richard. 2005. "Religious Convictions and Public Discourse." In Cuneo (2005): 195-216.
- Neuhaus. Richard. 1986. *The Naked Public Square*. Grand Rapids, MI: Eerdmans.
- Nussbaum, Martha. 2008. *Liberty of Conscience: In Defense of America's Tradition of Religious Equality*. New York: Perseus Books.
- Perry, Michael. 2006. *Toward a Theory of Human Rights: Religion, Law, Courts*. Cambridge University Press.
- ——. 2003. *Under God?* Cambridge University Press.
- ——. 1997. *Religion in Politics: Constitutional and Moral Perspectives*. Oxford University Press.
- ——. 1988. *Love and Power*. Oxford University Press.
- Quinn, Philip. 2005. "Can Christians Be Good Liberals?" In Andrew Chignell and Andrew Dole, eds., *God and the Ethics of Belief*. Cambridge University Press: 248-76.
- ——. 2005a. "Religion and Politics." In William E. Mann, ed. *The Blackwell Guide to the Philosophy of Religion*. Malden, MA: Blackwell: 305-29.
- ——. 2001. "Religious Citizens within the Limits of Public Reason." *The Modern Schoolman* 78: 105-24.
- ——. 1997. "Political Liberalisms and Their Exclusions of the Religious." In Weithman (1997): 138-61.
- Qutb, Sayyed. N.D. *Milestones*. Cedar Rapids, IA: The Mother Mosque Foundation.
- Rawls, John. 1997. "The Idea of Public Reason Revisited." *The University of Chicago Law Review* 64: 765-807.
- ——. 1993. *Political Liberalism*. New York: Columbia University Press.
- Rivera, Luis N. 1992. *A Violent Evangelism: The Political and Religious Conquest of the Americas* Louisville, KY: Westminster/John Knox Press.

- Rorty, Richard. 2003. "Religion in the Public Square: A Reconsideration." *Journal of Religious Ethics* 31: 141-49.

- ——. 1995. "Religion as Conversation-stopper." *Common Knowledge* 3: 1-6.

- Sandel, Michael. 2005. *Public Philosophy: Essays on Morality in Politics.* Cambridge, MA: Harvard University Press.

- Smith, Christian. 1998. *Evangelicalism: Embattled and Thriving.* University of Chicago Press.

- Smith, Steven B. 2006. *Reading Leo Strauss: Politics, Philosophy, Judaism.* University of Chicago Press.

- Strauss, Leo. 1997. "Preface to Hobbes politische Wissenshaft." In Kenneth Hart Green, ed. *Jewish Philosophy and the Crisis of Modernity.* Albany, NY: SUNY Press: 453-56.

- Smith, J. K. A. 2004. *Introducing Radical Orthodoxy.* Grand Rapids, MI: Baker Academic Press.

- Stout, Jeffrey. 2004. *Democracy and Tradition.* Princeton, NJ: Princeton University Press.

- Swaine, Lucas. 2006. *The Liberal Conscience: Politics and Principle in a World of Religious Pluralism.* New York: Columbia University Press.

- Swan, Kyle. 2007. "Law, Liberty, and Christian Morality." *Religious Studies* 43: 395-415.

- ——. 2006. "Can a Good Christian Be a Good Liberal?" *Public Affairs Quarterly* 20: 163-74.

- Tertullian. 2004. "To Scapula." In Alexander Roberts and James Donaldson, eds., *Ante-Nicene Fathers*, vol. 3. Peabody, MA: Hendrickson Publishers: 105-08.

- Weithman, Paul. 2007. "John Rawls's Idea of Public Reason: Two Questions." *Journal of Law, Philosophy and Culture* 1: 47-68.

- ——. 2002. *Religion and the Obligations of Citizenship.* Cambridge University Press.

- —— ed. 1997. *Religion and Contemporary Liberalism.* Notre Dame, IN: Notre Dame University Press.

- Wolterstorff, Nicholas. 2009. *Philosophical Essays on Politics and Religion*. Ed. Terence Cuneo. Oxford: Oxford University Press.
- ——. 2008. *Justice: Rights and Wrongs*. Princeton, NJ: Princeton University Press.
- ——. 2007. "The Paradoxical Role of Coercion in the Theory of Political Liberalism." *Journal of Law, Philosophy and Culture* 1: 101-25. Reprinted in Wolterstorff (2009).
- ——. 2006. "Abraham Kuyper." In John Witte, Jr. and Frank S. Alexander, eds., *The Teachings of Modern Christianity on Law, Politics, and Human Nature*, Vol. I. New York: Columbia University Press: 219-48. Reprinted in Wolterstorff (2009).
- ——. 2003. "An Engagement with Rorty." *Journal of Religious Ethics* 31:129-39. Reprinted in Wolterstorff (2009).
- ——. 2001. "Do Christians Have Good Reasons for Supporting Liberal Democracy?" *The Modern Schoolman* 78: 229-48. Reprinted in Wolterstorff (2009).
- ——. 2001. "A Religious Argument for the Civil Right to Freedom of Religious Exercise, Drawn from American History." *Wake Forest Law Review* 36: 535-556. Reprinted in Wolterstorff (2009).
- ——. 1997. "The Role of Religion in Decision and Discussion of Political Issues." In Robert Audi and Nicholas Wolterstorff. *Religion in the Public Square*. Lanham, MD: Rowman and Littlefield: 67-120.
- ——. 1997a. "Why We Should Reject What Liberalism Tells Us about Speaking and Acting in Public for Religious Reasons." In Weithman (1997): 162-81.
- ——. 2009a. "Why Can't We All Just Get Along with Each Other?" In Wolterstorff (2009).
- Zagorin, Perez. (2003). *How the Idea of Toleration Came to the West*. Princeton, NJ: Princeton University Press.
- Song, Sarah, "Multiculturalism", *The Stanford Encyclopedia of Philosophy (Winter 2010 Edition)*, Edward N. Zalta (ed.), URL = http://plato.stanford.edu/archives/win2010/entries/multiculturalism/

- Eberle, Chris and Cuneo, Terence, "Religion and Political Theory", *The Stanford Encyclopedia of Philosophy (Winter 2008 Edition)*, Edward N. Zalta (ed.), URL = http://plato.stanford.edu/archives/win2008/entries/religion-politics/